Praise for
The Prayer of Agur

"In Proverbs 30, Agur invites you to learn a simple prayer that will help you find your sweet spot in life. Thanks to Jay Payleitner for uncovering and unpacking this marvelous gem. Don't miss it."

> —Josh McDowell, international speaker, apologist, and author of more than one hundred books, including *More Than a Carpenter* and *Evidence That Demands a Verdict*

"In a world that calls us to the extremes of overabundance or minimalism, *The Prayer of Agur* leads us to a life of rested contentedness. Jay takes profound biblical wisdom and makes it accessible for normal people in everyday life. It is possible to find that God-ordained sweet spot, and Jay's treatment of Agur's prayer will show you how."

> —Jeff Vanderstelt, lead teaching pastor at Doxa Church and author of *Gospel Fluency*

"In his warm and familiar manner, Jay uses the Prayer of Agur to teach us the way to contentment. He genuinely addresses our push and pull against life's extremes and defines the path to balance. It's as though Jay's wisdom gleaned from this prayer gives us spiritual permission to be human and embrace the struggle, knowing it's normal, it's healthy, and it keeps us connected to the protection, direction, and provision of God as we lean into Him. This book is and will be a pivotal point in our walk with Christ now and for years to come."

—MARY ETHEL ECKARD, cofounder of Dragonfly
Ministries and author of *Lessons of a Dragonfly*

"Every verse of God's Word applies to our lives. But I must say, Agur's brief prayer in Proverbs 30 seems to have special significance to this generation. Thanks, Jay, for reminding us that we can live in God's will and it's a sweet place to be!"

—KEN BLANCHARD, coauthor of *The New One Minute Manager* and *Lead Like Jesus*

"What an awesome little book with a tremendous amount of wise advice from Agur, a lesser-known man who wrote one chapter in Proverbs. *The Prayer of Agur* made me realize the need for balance in my life in so many areas. A must-read."

—LINDA WILSON, guest coordinator for *Real Life*
on Cornerstone Network

"In a culture that celebrates extremes, *The Prayer of Agur* is a clarion call back to the 'sweet spot of knowing Jesus.' Jay reminds us that even at the time of Creation, God Himself knew when to stop."

—MARK HANCOCK, CEO of Trail Life USA and author
of *Why Are We Sitting Here Until We Die?*, *Let Boys
Be Boys,* and *5 Critical Needs of Boys*

"In *The Prayer of Agur,* Jay will help you find the balance between too much and too little so you can enjoy a more fulfilling and purposeful life. You'll discover through this delightful read that it really is possible to trust God to provide exactly what you need and to live in the sweet spot of His best for you."

—CINDI MCMENAMIN, author of *When God Sees Your Tears* and *Drama Free*

"This book is at once poetically written and powerfully rich as it illuminates Agur's motives and prayer, which accurately reflect our own hearts' longings. Instead of wondering whether I've identified God's perfect will and agonizing over every decision, now I'm finding His sweet spot for my life!"

—CAESAR KALINOWSKI, missional strategist and coach and author of *The Gospel Primer*

"The saying 'The greatest gifts come in small packages' is certainly true about this small book. Jay Payleitner and Agur are quite a team as together they examine the most important things in life, the fears that hold us back, and the possibility of a life joyfully lived in the discovery of a new perspective."

—PHYLLIS HENDRY HALVERSON, president and CEO of Lead Like Jesus

Books by Jay Payleitner

Day-by-Day Devotions for Dads
What If God Wrote Your Shopping List?
The Jesus Dare
Love Notes from God
What If God Wrote Your To-Do List?
If God Were Your Life Coach
Lifeology
52 Ways to Connect as a Couple
What If God Wrote Your Bucket List?
52 Things Sons Need from Their Dads
If God Wrote Your Birthday Card
52 Things Husbands Need from Their Wives
52 Things Daughters Need from Their Dads
If God Gave Your Graduation Speech
Do Something Beautiful
52 Things Wives Need from Their Husbands
365 Ways to Say "I Love You" to Your Kids
52 Things Kids Need from a Dad
The One Year Life Verse Devotional
Once Upon a Tandem

the PRAYER of AGUR

Ancient Wisdom for Discovering
Your Sweet Spot in Life

Jay Payleitner

MULTNOMAH

Hardcover ISBN 978-0-525-65383-7
eBook ISBN 978-0-525-65384-4

Published in the United States by Multnomah, an imprint of Random House, a division of Penguin Random House LLC.

MULTNOMAH® and its mountain colophon are registered trademarks of Penguin Random House LLC.

Library of Congress Cataloging-in-Publication Data
Names: Payleitner, Jay K., author.
Title: The prayer of Agur : ancient wisdom for discovering your sweet spot in life / Jay Payleitner.
Description: First edition. | Colorado Springs : Multnomah, 2020. | Includes bibliographical references.
Identifiers: LCCN 2019026445 | ISBN 9780525653837 (hardcover) | ISBN 9780525653844 (ebook)
Subjects: LCSH: Agur (Biblical figure) | Bible. Proverbs, XXX, 7–9—Criticism, interpretation, etc. | Prayer—Biblical teaching.
Classification: LCC BS1465.52 .P39 2020 | DDC 223/.706—dc23
LC record available at https://lccn.loc.gov/2019026445

Printed in the United States of America
2020—First Edition

10 9 8 7 6 5 4 3 2 1

SPECIAL SALES
Most Multnomah books are available at special quantity discounts when purchased in bulk by corporations, organizations, and special-interest groups. Custom imprinting or excerpting can also be done to fit special needs. For information, please email specialmarketscms @penguinrandomhouse.com.

To Alec, Lindsay, Randall, Rachel,
Max, Megan, Isaac, Kaitlin, and Rae Anne.
I pray you continue to seek, find,
and live in God's sweet spot.

Give me neither poverty nor riches,
but give me only my daily bread.

—PROVERBS 30:8

Contents

Note to the Reader

Dear Reader,

Are you, like me, caught in the middle? Being pulled in two directions? Some days, we want more. More opportunities. More responsibilities. And, yes, more stuff. Other days, we want less. Fewer distractions. Fewer responsibilities. Less stuff to take care of and worry about.

We're either energized or exhausted. Confident or reluctant. Spiritually in tune or entertaining doubts.

Allow me to introduce you to Agur. He's the guy inspired by God to unscramble this exact conundrum. Agur's commonsensical approach to life and his strangely amusing chapter near the end of the book of Proverbs reveal how you already might be in the center of God's will. That's a wonderful place to be. Especially in today's turbulent culture.

Join me as we consider living in God's sweet spot. Finding a balance between too much and too little. Inviting Him to simply love us where we are. And knowing we can trust Him to provide exactly what we need.

Warmly,
Jay Payleitner

Introduction

You picked up this small book—and I wrote it—because of the allure of a short prayer hidden in plain sight in the book of Proverbs. It reads easily. Speaks honestly. And contains a nice little unexpected twist. Here it is:

> Two things I ask of you, LORD;
>   do not refuse me before I die:
> Keep falsehood and lies far from me;
>   give me neither poverty nor riches,
>   but give me only my daily bread.
> Otherwise, I may have too much and disown you
>   and say, "Who is the LORD?"
> Or I may become poor and steal,
>   and so dishonor the name of my God. (30:7–9)

Read it again. And maybe a third time.

Did you get it? There's a chance you did. Totally. Message received. If that's the case, you can put this book back on the shelf and move on to your next theological brainteaser. For savvy people like you, this passage is fairly straightforward.

Or is it?

I submit there's more to the Prayer of Agur and the surrounding passages than you might imagine. There's quite a bit of subtext and tons of application for today. So before you go, allow me to tease you with a few unexpected observations regarding Agur and his contribution to one of the most quoted books of the Bible.

First, Agur's prayer is the *only* prayer in all of Proverbs. Considering the many topics covered and the literary devices included in the book of Proverbs, that should come as a bit of a surprise.

Second, while there are hundreds of prophecies in the Old Testament predicting Jesus as the coming Messiah, the chapter written by Agur is one of a handful of times where the idea of God *having a son* is actually mentioned (see verse 4). It turns out Agur was more than just a guy who wrote commonsense prayers. He was a true prophet.

Third, Agur's short yet powerful prayer is especially applicable today. Too many individuals, families, churches, and communities are trapped in a cycle of self-destructive behavior including lying to ourselves, lying to others, chasing wealth, and fearing poverty. The twenty-first-century life is way out of balance, careening between extremes. Agur is praying desperately to see the big picture and live in that sweet spot of knowing Jesus, knowing He is enough, and knowing He's got a plan for our lives.

Finally, I hope you will stay with me and dig deep into Proverbs 30 *in its entirety*. All thirty-three verses. The words of Agur could very well leave you with a new perspective on the perks of humility, the dark side of hypocrisy, and the eternal rewards of trusting God. Plus, you also will be invited to ponder how ants can carry so much weight, why lizards sneak into castles, and how snakes slither. Sound like fun?

As promised by the title, this book is mostly about a prayer. But like every prayer, there's a story behind it. That story is well worth uncovering.

Moving forward, we're going to go line by line through this second-to-last chapter of Proverbs and unearth what little we know about this fellow named Agur.

- First, we'll look at the six verses that build a platform for Agur's prayer.
- Then we'll spend some extra time properly examining verses 7–9, which contain that paradoxical petition.
- After the prayer, Agur turns the wordplay up a notch by presenting five short, peculiar lists that make the second half of the chapter feel more like a television game show than Scripture.
- Finally, we'll close with an unexpected bonus that comes with living in God's sweet spot. It's a gift you don't want to miss.

So stick around. This small book delivers a big message. When you've finished, share it with a few like-minded friends, questioning seekers, or skeptical cynics. See if their impressions and takeaways match yours. Let's get this party started.

What Is a Sweet Spot?

Tennis players know there is a sweet spot on their racket where the ball jumps off the nylon strings with maximum velocity and precision. When that happens, there's no vibration in their hand and the ball travels straight and true.

The same is true of baseball bats and vocal performances. You'll hear players say things like, "It was a fast ball down the middle, and it found the sweet spot of my bat." Or vocalists might say, "I love that song. It's really in my sweet spot."

Career counselors will describe your sweet spot as the job where your gifts and passions intersect with the needs of the marketplace. In other words, doing what you love, doing it well, and getting paid for it.

Likewise, there is a way God wants you to live. Where you're living with purpose, not futility. Where your senses garner clarity, not chaos. It's not running too fast or too slow. It's not amassing a fortune or living in squalor.

You'll find your sweet spot when you have a sense of belonging because you know God loves you for who you are, not what you do. Sound good?

Major Impact from a Minor Character

Allow me to introduce a man I am quite confident will be a new friend, colleague, and favorite author. His name is Agur. He's smart, funny, and quite perceptive. He loves God. He's streetwise in a good way. And he's not afraid to speak his mind.

Agur recognizes there is much he does not know. But he asks good questions. He will occasionally interrupt himself right in the middle of a stream of thoughtful teaching to deliver a seemingly random but enlightening truth we all need to hear. His writings make for quite a wild ride.

Somehow, Agur's writings made their way into the book of Proverbs. You have to give him credit for that. Three millennia ago there were quite a few word-slingers filling papyrus scrolls with inspired ruminations. Being included in the Old Testament alongside kings, prophets, and other spiritual giants is quite a coup.

Bible scholars agree that Solomon personally wrote or compiled chapters 1 through 29 of Proverbs. But how and why the last two chapters were tacked on is a bit of a mystery. No one disputes their relevance or authenticity, but very little is known about the authors.

We do know that Lemuel, author of chapter 31, was a king who received wise teaching from his mother. King Lemuel's celebrated description in verses 10–31 of a "wife of noble character" has helped keep that last chapter of Proverbs in the limelight. The "Proverbs 31 woman" is a popular theme at women's events.

Even less is known about Agur, author of chapter 30. As indicated in the opening words of the chapter, he was the son of Jakeh, another obscure reference, and he may have been from northern Arabia.[1] That's all the history we have. I suspect most readers of the Bible have never spent more than a moment considering his name, his reputation, or his single puzzling appearance in Scripture. Actually, that's not unusual. There are quite a few historical characters who show up for a single scene or have only the briefest mention in the Bible but still leave a memorable impression. To prove the point, let's take a quick look at three of them.

There's Simeon, the aging prophet who met Mary and Joseph at the temple in Jerusalem when they presented Jesus soon after the fortieth day following His birth. The Holy Spirit had promised Simeon he would not die before seeing the Messiah. Taking the infant in his arms, the old man prophesied that Jesus would be a light to the world, causing the fall and rise of many people. His memorable story takes up a mere eleven verses in Luke 2.

The name Jochebed is mentioned only twice—both times in long genealogies. But we could make the case that her actions *launched* biblical history. The mother of three heroes of the faith—Moses, Aaron, and Miriam—Jochebed had the foresight and courage to send three-month-old Moses floating down the Nile in a papyrus basket to rescue him from Egyptian death squads (see Exodus 1–2). We may not remember her name, but she should be revered as a beacon of hope for anyone living under oppression and for mothers who love their children enough to let them go.

A third unforgettable biblical character mentioned ever so briefly is the repentant thief on the cross. On that history-changing Friday at Golgotha, one criminal hurled abusive taunts at Jesus, but the other recognized the divinity of Christ and confessed his own brokenness. We don't know his name, but that thief's insight at the triple crucifixion brings hope to those who come to Christ late in life, even in their final moments. In addition, Jesus's promise to the thief, "Truly I tell you, today you will be with me in paradise" (Luke 23:43), suggests there is no lag time between our time on earth and our entrance into heaven. That's good to know.

It's also good to know that modest lives like yours and mine can still make an impact. Can you identify with a guy who was moved to tears when he held a new baby, a mother who saw a great leader when she looked at her infant son, or someone whose eyes were opened upon meeting Jesus for the first time? Like Agur, these were real people. Simeon, Jochebed, and the thief on the cross were simply doing life.

On the other hand, the larger-than-life characters in the Bible—like Noah, Moses, Elijah, Abraham, David, Paul—can be a bit difficult to relate to. After all, God spoke to them on multiple occasions, and the Bible chronicles significant portions of their lives. That's why, when I first came across Proverbs 30, I knew I had found an ally in Agur, a fellow humble traveler on this road of life.

I appreciate that Agur's sayings—all thirty-three verses of Proverbs 30—made the cut. Since the chapter *is* included, then clearly the Bible would be incomplete without it! Which means we have a responsibility to spend time reflecting on how Agur's words apply to our lives.

What's more, his voice and his message desperately need to be heard today by anyone who longs for a like-minded friend and a dose of reality.

A Note to Skeptics, Cynics, and Seekers

In his chapter—and especially in his prayer—Agur admits he doesn't have all the answers and asks for help. He confesses that falsehoods occasionally flow from his mouth. He can't always discern between the truth and lies he hears from others. He knows he needs a certain cash flow, but he doesn't want too much or too little.

The idea that a prophet and contributor to the Bible lives with a bit of angst and uncertainty should be a comfort. In this life, it's okay if we don't have all the answers. God welcomes our doubts and questions. Jesus said, "Whoever comes to me I will never cast out" (John 6:37, ESV) and, "Come to me, all you who are weary and burdened, and I will give you rest" (Matthew 11:28).

Like us, Agur has all kinds of questions and makes many quirky observations. That's why Proverbs 30 is so engaging. Agur is the real deal, flaws and all.

The Bible is filled with people who make mistakes, turn to God, find answers, and then still attempt to do life under their own power. Thankfully, God's love overrides their failures . . . and ours.

So bring your doubts, questions, fears, and suspicions. God is big enough to handle them. You won't hurt His feelings. After all, He knows them anyway.

2

Utterance from a Collector

The sayings of Agur son of Jakeh—an inspired utterance.

This man's utterance to Ithiel:

"I am weary, God,
   but I can prevail.
Surely I am only a brute, not a man;
   I do not have human understanding.
I have not learned wisdom,
   nor have I attained to the knowledge of the Holy One."

—Proverbs 30:1–3

A dmittedly, I was drawn to find out more about Agur and study his words because of the sixty-four-word prayer included in the only chapter of the Bible attributed to him. I promise we'll dig deep into the message of that prayer in a few pages. In the meantime, as suggested by most theologians when studying a specific passage, let's consider the context. This means we're going to look at a bit of history, consider the derivational meaning of some names, and delve into the six verses before the prayer and the twenty-four verses after.

In most study Bibles, chapter 30 of Proverbs is titled "Sayings of Agur" or "Words of Agur." Straightaway, verse 1 presents three names: Agur, Jakeh, and Ithiel. At this point, you won't be surprised to hear that *none* of these individuals are mentioned elsewhere in Scripture.

In Hebrew, the name Agur can be translated as "collector."[2] Which should lead you to ask, What did Agur collect? As you will discover, he was a list maker. The short lists he includes in the second half of his chapter are the kind of deep thoughts with an ironic twist you might expect from a standup comedian specializing in observational humor. You might say Agur was a collector of ideas and questions, which ultimately he would share with the world.

In later chapters in this book, we'll take a close look at those amusing, confusing, and thought-provoking lists. If you're anything like me, you will appreciate Agur's quirky take on life. For now, let's continue to explore Proverbs 30:1.

The name of Agur's father, Jakeh, comes from an Arabic root meaning "carefully religious."[3] If I may speculate, it's possible that Agur's father would get caught up in scrutinizing the complexity and subtext of every papyrus scroll lying around the temple or every word passed down by word of mouth from the days of Abraham, the Exodus, judges, and kings. Being carefully religious can be a healthy pursuit, unless getting caught up in details prevents you from applying God's truth to your life today. I think I prefer the approach taken by Jakeh's slightly rebellious son, Agur, who uses down-to-earth common sense to observe and reveal the obvious.

After reviewing his personal lineage, Agur introduces us to his audience: Ithiel. Scholars translate that name as "God is with me."[4] It could be that Agur sought out Ithiel as someone with godly insight who might be able to answer his many questions. But you'll notice that at this point Agur doesn't speak with great confidence or authority. He delivers a mere utterance that suggests some hesitation or searching for the right words. He admits to being weary but still aspires to say something worth saying. "I can prevail," he writes with a hint of hopeful desperation.

In the verses that follow, our new friend powers through his weariness to formulate some perceptive questions. Still, there's a disarming and welcome humility about his approach. Agur is the refreshing opposite of those slick, vainglorious preachers who claim to have all the answers to every question.

Personally, I prefer to listen to a Bible teacher who acknowledges his need for a savior. Someone who tells self-deprecating stories and admits he has "not learned wisdom." Agur even admits he is brutish or beastly, almost subhuman! Until he meets God face to face, Agur concedes that he has not "attained to the knowledge of the Holy One" (verse 3).

The takeaway from the first three verses written by Agur might be that human wisdom is faulty. Even those who are "carefully religious" or are identified as being "with God" should admit they are starving for answers.

With that as a starting point, Agur suddenly begins posing questions worth asking.

Agur Asks Questions Worth Asking

Who has gone up to heaven and come down?
   Whose hands have gathered up the wind?
Who has wrapped up the waters in a cloak?
   Who has established all the ends of the earth?
What is his name, and what is the name of his son?
   Surely you know!

—PROVERBS 30:4

A s Agur begins verse 4, he speaks with clarity and conviction, asking six excellent questions:

"Who has visited heaven?"

"Who gathers the wind?"

"Who controls the seas?"

"Who made the earth?"

"What is his name?"

"What is the name of his son?"

Then he answers his own questions, saying, "Surely you know!"

You have to love his confidence. It's the same confidence expressed in Psalm 19:1: "The heavens declare the glory of God." Agur is acknowledging that his confidence comes from something beyond himself. He's confirming that anyone who considers the wonder of nature—the wind, the seas, the size and scope of the earth—must acknowledge the Creator.

In the New Testament, that confidence is reinforced and taken a step further. Romans 1:20 tells us, "Since the creation of the world God's invisible qualities—his eternal power and divine nature—

have been clearly seen, being understood from what has been made, so that people are without excuse."

In other words, the creation proves there is a Creator. There really isn't any excuse for not coming to that conclusion. People who think otherwise are probably a little too distracted with their own personal accomplishments to see God's accomplishments.

Going back to verse 3, Agur has just confessed that he doesn't have "knowledge of the Holy One." In verse 4, he explains why. Agur has been busy pondering the source of creation, deliberating about who or what controls the universe. Agur is asking big questions. As a mere human, he realizes there's no way he can wrap his head around those questions. Then he lands on the obvious answer. "Surely you know!" he tells his audience with exceeding confidence. Indeed. Surely anyone who has ever contemplated the heavens, the seas, or the scope of the planet knows that God is large and in charge.

While the first four questions center on the idea of creation, the next two bombshells take on the task of identifying who is in control. "What is his name?" and "What is the name of his son?"

Keep in mind that Agur's writings appear in the middle of the Old Testament. As he asked those questions, a great number of names for the Creator of the universe had already been established, including Yahweh (I Am or Lord), El Shaddai (God Almighty), El Elyon (God Most High), Adonai (Lord), and Jehovah Jireh (the Lord Will Provide).

After expressing a dose of humility, Agur reveals a firm grasp on God's sovereignty. His confidence establishes a foundation for the sincere prayer he will be presenting in just a few more words. By asking "What is his name?" he confirms that not only is God worth praising but even His *name* is glorious. Just as we are commanded in Deuteronomy 28:58, His "glorious and awesome name" must be revered.

Then comes Agur's sixth question, "What is the name of his son?" Even though it is a question, it delivers an unexpected insight that probably sent shock waves through the cedar-lined halls of Solomon's temple. *This dude is proclaiming to the world that God has a Son!*

When the book of Proverbs came together, anyone paying close attention to the writings of the prophets would have seen scores of verses foreshadowing the coming Messiah. But there had been only *three* references that the Messiah would be the Son of God.

One stirring description of God's future Son comes in 2 Samuel when the Lord speaks to David, through the prophet Nathan, in the night. Can you imagine the voice of God?

When your days are over and you rest with your ancestors,
I will raise up your offspring to succeed you, your own flesh
and blood, and I will establish his kingdom. He is the one
who will build a house for my Name, and I will establish the
throne of his kingdom forever. I will be his father, and he will
be my son. When he does wrong, I will punish him with a rod

wielded by men, with floggings inflicted by human hands.
But my love will never be taken away from him. (7:12–15)

Did you see it? God is saying, "I will be his father, and he will
be my son." That's an earth-shattering promise. Bible scholars see
this passage as a multilayered prophecy that points to Solomon, son
of David, building the temple and to the Messiah, Son of God,
building the kingdom of heaven.

We find the other two early references to God's sending His
Son to live among us in Psalms 2 and 89.

I will proclaim the LORD's decree:

He said to me, "You are my son;
    today I have become your father.
Ask me, and I will make the nations your inheritance,
    the ends of the earth your possession.
You will break them with a rod of iron;
    you will dash them to pieces like pottery."

Therefore, you kings, be wise;
    be warned, you rulers of the earth.
Serve the LORD with fear
    and celebrate his rule with trembling.
Kiss his son, or he will be angry
    and your way will lead to your destruction. (2:7–12)

My faithfulness and unfailing love will be with him,
 and by my authority he will grow in power.
I will extend his rule over the sea,
 his dominion over the rivers.
And he will call out to me, "You are my Father,
 my God, and the Rock of my salvation."
I will make him my firstborn son,
 the mightiest king on earth.
I will love him and be kind to him forever;
 my covenant with him will never end. (89:24–28, NLT)

Theologians have counted more than four hundred messianic prophecies in the Old Testament that point to the birth, life, death, resurrection, and teachings of Jesus Christ. But only the three cited above mention God's Son *and* predate Agur.

You can find additional references to the coming Son of God in the Old Testament books of Isaiah, Daniel, Hosea, and Micah,[5] but those came well after Agur put his pen to papyrus.

Personally, I think it's remarkable that our often-overlooked friend Agur was one of the first in history to acknowledge that the forthcoming King of kings would be God's one and only Son. Don't you?

In Proverbs 30:4, we've made note that Agur asks six questions. Regarding questions one through five, his emphatic response, "Surely you know!" was quite accurate. His contemporaries would immediately know Agur was pointing to God, our heavenly Father. But that last question—"What is the name of his son?"—was a stumper. It wouldn't be answered for around nine hundred years. Is that a contradiction? An error in Scripture? Hardly. The Bible delivers eternal truth. It's written for people then, now, and years from now. The members of Agur's ancient audience may have been a bit perplexed since they would not have known the name of Jesus—but such is the nature of prophecy. Readers of those words *today* surely smile when they read that passage. After all, you and I assuredly do know the name of God's Son.[6]

THE NAME ABOVE EVERY OTHER NAME

Interestingly, the name Jesus never appears in English translations of the Old Testament, although the Hebrew name Yeshua means "deliverer" and "savior" and can be translated in Greek to the name Jesus. The name Joshua is also linked to Yeshua. (The English spelling of Jesus didn't appear until the seventeenth century, amid quite a bit of controversy. But that's a story for another day.)

The name Jesus does appear in the very first verse of the New Testament, appropriately introducing the ancestral record of the promised Messiah: "This is the genealogy of Jesus the Messiah the son of David, the son of Abraham" (Matthew 1:1).

4

Agur Takes a Moment to Endorse Scripture

Every word of God is flawless;

    he is a shield to those who take refuge in him.

Do not add to his words,

    or he will rebuke you and prove you a liar.

—Proverbs 30:5–6

After establishing his humility and stunning his audience with insight about God and His Son, Agur provides another ironic twist to his prose. He writes, "Every word of God is flawless" and "Do not add to his words."

The paradox is that those statements from Agur are included in the pages of God's Word, which means Agur's words are flawless only because they have been added to God's Word, which is expressly forbidden in Agur's words.

Confused? Well, don't be. The Bible was written by men but inspired by God. That happened only because the writers were inspired in the moment by the Holy Spirit. So when Agur wrote those words, he was *already* speaking from God. That concept is explained well in 2 Peter 1:20–21: "Above all, you must realize that no prophecy in Scripture ever came from the prophet's own understanding, or from human initiative. No, those prophets were moved by the Holy Spirit, and they spoke from God" (NLT).

What's more, there's infinite value in all Scripture, including the passages written by our obscure and thought-provoking friend

Agur. In 2 Timothy 3:16 we are promised, "All Scripture is God-breathed and is useful for teaching, rebuking, correcting and training in righteousness."

The fact that we are debating and deciphering the meaning of Proverbs 30 should not bring concern. Interpreting God's Word—and sometimes getting it wrong—is a long-standing tradition for scholars, seekers, high priests, and God's chosen people.

Need examples?

Moses brought the Ten Commandments down from Mount Sinai, and the Israelites rejected them. In their old age, Sarah and Abraham scoffed when God told them they would have a son. Their joy was revealed when they named their baby Isaac, which means "laughter."[7] The Pharisees famously mocked the words of Jesus. Throughout biblical history, men of authentic faith such as Job, Gideon, and Thomas all expressed doubts.

Agur's warning in verse 6, that anyone adding to God's words will be rebuked, foreshadows one of the last verses of the Bible. Revelation 22:18 promises, "If anyone adds anything to what is written here, God will add to that person the plagues described in this book" (NLT).

All that to say, God's Word can, does, and should stand on its own. It's quite common for Bible scholars to insist, "The Bible proves the Bible is true." Now, you might think a statement like that would open the door for all kinds of scoffing. Skeptics might say, "That's like a judge presiding over his own trial" or "That's the same as when a dictator gets elected by allowing only one name on the ballot." It might even seem like a fair question to ask, "How can the Bible prove the Bible?"

But what those skeptics haven't considered is that some forty authors from very different backgrounds contributed to the Bible over approximately fifteen hundred years. Those sixty-six ancient books are part of a whole, but each can also be judged on its own merit. The Bible is an intricate tapestry of poetry, stories, history, and laws. Despite what you may have heard, it contains no contradictions. Scholars much smarter than I am can point to all kinds of evidence for its reliability. Ancient manuscripts supporting its authenticity, archaeological discoveries, fulfilled prophecies, eyewitness histories, and an unending archive of broken lives completely healed by God's Word should be enough. But some folks need more.

To that group, I would say the Bible itself understands where you're coming from. To authentic Christians, the glory of God is astoundingly self-evident, but if you aren't in tune with the Holy Spirit, you shouldn't expect to see it. Paul wrote, "The person without the Spirit does not accept the things that come from the Spirit of God but considers them foolishness, and cannot understand them because they are discerned only through the Spirit" (1 Corinthians 2:14).

In his own way, Agur was saying, "God is eager and able to give you refuge from all the crud of this world and the next. If you go your own way or make up your own religion, you will suffer the consequences. But that's your choice."

Agur is confirming that the Bible speaks truth to everyone on the planet who is willing to listen. God's love also extends to every soul. But God's *protection* applies only to those who have surrendered to Him.

You'll note that Agur doesn't spend much time at all defending the Bible. He just wants to make sure—before he begins his from-the-heart prayer—that you know where he stands.

5

Agur's Prayer, Part I

Regarding Lies Coming and Going

Two things I ask of you, Lord;
 do not refuse me before I die:
Keep falsehood and lies far from me.

—Proverbs 30:7–8

R eady? We're about to enter the nuts and bolts of Proverbs 30. Agur begins his three-verse prayer with a promise to keep his request short. Just two items. He writes, "Two things I ask of you, LORD."

That's a good strategy for prayer. If we drone on and on with a long list of complaints, frustrations, and requests, we're going to start adding items we don't really need, plus we'll have a hard time tracking God's response. For sure, when you pray, God has already heard your prayer and formulated His loving and perfect response. It's also true that it would be impossible to give God more than He can handle. You could list a million petitions and He would answer every single one. But considering our own *human* limitations, maybe we need to slow down and pray more simply, thoughtfully, and intentionally.

To be clear, the Bible does teach us to "pray without ceasing" (1 Thessalonians 5:17, ESV) and even to "pray in the Spirit at all times and on every occasion. Stay alert and be persistent in your prayers for all believers everywhere" (Ephesians 6:18, NLT).

But we're also supposed to be prudent and reverent in our

prayer life: "Devote yourselves to prayer, being watchful and thankful" (Colossians 4:2).

Similarly, we shouldn't evaluate prayer strictly on the quantity of words. You can offer a quick prayer anytime and anywhere, but in general, prayer should never be flurried or hurried: "When you pray, do not keep on babbling like pagans, for they think they will be heard because of their many words" (Matthew 6:7).

Prayer is all about sincerity and humility, followed by listening and responding: "If my people, who are called by my name, will humble themselves and pray and seek my face and turn from their wicked ways, then I will hear from heaven, and I will forgive their sin and will heal their land" (2 Chronicles 7:14).

Anytime you can boil your prayer down to a small number of specific heartfelt desires—as modeled by our friend Agur—you're going to find yourself more aware of God working in you and through you to deliver answers.

What two things does Agur ask for? After thinking it through, he has identified his top two most hazardous personal weaknesses. The two things he struggles with most: discerning truth and owning stuff. Let's tackle one at a time.

Agur prays, "Keep falsehoods and lies far from me." You can almost hear Agur's thought process and expanded prayer, as if he's saying, *I know the world is filled with lies, and they trip me up way too often. Father in heaven, please protect my ears from hearing lies that might lead me down the wrong path. And keep my lips from lying so that I might not deceive others.*

I think Agur is onto something. Truth matters. Whether it's input or output, whether we are hearing it or speaking it, there is truth and we can know it. It sets us free. Ignore truth, and bad decisions result. Satan, the father of lies, has been obscuring truth since the Garden of Eden, and we know how that turned out.

An excellent example of disregarding truth comes from Pontius Pilate, the wishy-washy Roman governor of Judea who couldn't make up his mind about what to do with Jesus. In John 18:37–38, he asks Jesus a series of questions attempting to discern whether Jesus had really claimed to be king. Jesus responds, "You say that I am a king. In fact, the reason I was born and came into the world is to testify to the truth. Everyone on the side of truth listens to me."

Pilate scoffs, "What is truth?"

If Pilate had been paying closer attention, he would have known that the man he was about to sentence to death was truth incarnate. Jesus was God's promise of love, hope, faith, and virtue in human form.

Curiously, Pilate suggested more than once that Jesus was innocent, but he caved in to public pressure. Once you start denying the existence of truth, then every decision you make will be without a firm foundation. That's a warning we all might heed.

Part 1 of Agur's prayer is a sincere brokenness before the Creator of the universe. Somehow he knows the destructive consequences of falsehoods and lies. He recognizes that Satan—even though he is a master deceiver—can't stand up to virtue and integrity. Agur wants to be on the winning team. That comes from hearing truth, discerning truth, and speaking truth.

The three short opening lines of Agur's prayer also foreshadow one of the key instructions Jesus would give regarding prayer during the Sermon on the Mount: "Lead us not into temptation, but deliver us from the evil one" (Matthew 6:13).

Agur's Prayer, Part II

Not Too Much, Not Too Little

Give me neither poverty nor riches,
but give me only my daily bread.

—Proverbs 30:8

The beginning of Agur's prayer is a personal request that he would give and receive only truth. That's extraordinary but not surprising. After all, everyone wants to know what's really true; even liars know lying is wrong.

However, Agur's next request is a stunner. He dares to pray for a life of moderation: "Give me neither poverty nor riches, but give me only my daily bread."

Moderation? That's not on anyone's checklist, especially in the twenty-first century. We are living in an age of extremes.

For most people, bigger will always be better. More house. More car. More closet space. More shelves for more trophies. More activities. More responsibility so you can gain more of the above.

On the flip side is another extreme: a subculture of people—even entire communities—who are choosing to live as minimalists. It's not a new phenomenon, but minimalism has recently made its way into the public eye. Maybe you know people who are mildly obsessed with cutting up credit cards and clearing out clutter. They eschew the latest gadgets, and their entire wardrobe fits in one cardboard box and a knapsack. Their expressed goals include napping more and living 100 percent debt-free. They are conspicuously moving into micro apartments and tiny homes.

Committed minimalists pause before purchasing and practice the "one in, one out" rule, which means they don't buy something new without getting rid of something they no longer need or use.

Some social scientists suggest that the practice of minimalism is a response to the unabashed consumerism that exploded after World War II. The men and women who grew up in the Great Depression and lived during World War II came to be known as the greatest generation. When they started their own families, these men and women were the first to buy televisions, second cars, and houses in the suburbs. Suddenly "faster" was ubiquitous, as evidenced by the introduction of interstate highways, commercial jet airlines, direct-dial telephones, and fast-food restaurants.

Don't be mistaken: that generation—mostly departed—was not motivated by greed. They were all about building a better life for their families. Quite nobly, they wanted their kids to have and achieve more than they did growing up. Unfortunately, they couldn't anticipate the consequences of their ambitions.

Any student of recent history will tell you—two or three generations later—that evidence reveals that bigger, faster, busier, and pricier might *not* be better. Without listing the multiple ways that society is broken, suffice it to say it's not uncommon for bigger, faster, busier, and pricier to lead to heartbreak and despair. When we consider the ramifications of overspending, overconsuming, and overindulging, there is ample justification for the minimalist mind-set.

Still, Agur is not endorsing minimalism. Nor is he suggesting that wealth and influence define success. He endorses neither fast nor slow, big nor small, fancy nor simple.

Our endearing friend Agur has identified a sweet spot: the perfect balance of getting what you need and needing what you get. He sums it up nicely: "my daily bread."

Any of Agur's peers who heard this prayer would instantly connect this request to the daily manna God had provided to their ancestors as they wandered the desert for forty years as described in Exodus. Manna appeared once a day, provided by God in just the right amount at just the right time.

As twenty-first-century readers, we recognize the phrase "give us this day our daily bread" from the Lord's Prayer, delivered almost a thousand years later by Jesus in His Sermon on the Mount.

The words are comfortable, and we nod our heads. *Yes, Lord, please meet our daily needs.*

The thing is, that's not what Agur prayed. He added the word *only.* That introduces an entirely deeper level of trust in the One who provides.

Raise your hand if you have the courage to say that portion of Agur's prayer, "Give me *only* my daily bread."

Why, by the way, would anyone pray that way? The next chapter unpacks the last portion of Agur's prayer and presents two good reasons.

Agur's Prayer, Part III

Possible Repercussions of Living in the Extremes

Otherwise, I may have too much and disown you
and say, "Who is the LORD?"
Or I may become poor and steal,
and so dishonor the name of my God.

—PROVERBS 30:9

Do you know your weaknesses? Have you considered when and where you are most vulnerable to temptation? Agur—a bright guy who had a lot going for him—identified the chink in his armor. It was greed. This passage reveals that he was well aware he had trouble dealing with money. His personal obsession over his cash flow was his Achilles' heel. He knew that too much or too little could easily distract him. Even destroy him.

To be clear, money itself was not the problem. It was Agur's emotional attachment to money. That idea foretells the oft-quoted (and misquoted) warning from the New Testament: "The love of money is the root of all kinds of evil" (1 Timothy 6:10, NLT).

It's worth noting that many reference this verse but leave off the first three words. Paul was not saying money breeds evil. Rather, it's the *love* of money that causes all kinds of evil. What kinds of evil? While there are no specifics in that passage, it does describe how "some people, craving money, have wandered from the true faith and pierced themselves with many sorrows" (verse 10, NLT).

Once again, let's applaud the self-awareness displayed by our friend Agur. He is praying, in essence, "Lord, keep me dependent on You. Having complete trust in You is the sweet spot in which I want to live. I can't do life without You."

Agur is not just being humble—he has thought this request through! If he has too much, he knows how he will react. He will think, *Maybe I don't need God after all.* This man who contributed a single chapter to the Old Testament was foreshadowing Jesus's warning in Mark 10:25: "It is easier for a camel to go through the eye of a needle than for someone who is rich to enter the kingdom of God."

Agur also realizes that if he has too little, his physical hunger will likely override his integrity. He will steal food and get caught, and God's name will be dragged through the mud. Agur knows the Ten Commandments, confirms that the one prohibiting stealing is still valid, and accepts that stealing is punishable by the courts and by God.

Having more than we need. Having less than we need. Both extremes are lose-lose. But somewhere in between is that beautiful concept known as contentment.

Is that something you can pray for? Can you pray to have neither too little nor too much? Can you pray for *just right*?

If having just enough becomes one of your top priorities, you'll find plenty of additional biblical support.

I know what it is to be in need, and I know what it is to have plenty. I have learned the secret of being content in any and every situation, whether well fed or hungry, whether living in plenty or in want. I can do all this through him who gives me strength. (Philippians 4:12–13)

Godliness with contentment is great gain. (1 Timothy 6:6)

Better a little with the fear of the LORD than great wealth with turmoil. (Proverbs 15:16)

Now let's move beyond Agur's temptations and vulnerabilities and talk about yours.

Perhaps greed isn't a problem for you. Congratulations! But beyond greed, what about sloth, envy, anger, pride, lust, and gluttony? Commonly called the seven deadly sins, these vices are not listed in the Bible.[8] But they can be a helpful place to start when choosing to do a self-examination of what's broken in your life.

Without getting too personal, let's imagine you have an anger issue. The smallest frustration tends to set you off on a rampage. You know it's a problem, and you've asked God to take away your rage. But you also don't want to be a complete pushover because there are many issues in our world that merit a healthy dose of righteous anger. Can you imagine yourself praying the following?

Give me neither furious rage nor vapid cowardice,
    but give me a consistent sense of composure.
Otherwise, I may wimp out and allow injustices to prevail

and say, "Where is the Lord?"
Or I may lose my cool,
     and so dishonor the name of my God.

Although this is my own adaptation of Agur's prayer, can you see how there might be a sweet spot for the emotion of anger? That would mean saving your wrath for the right time to make the right point to the right people. I think Agur would approve of that plan.

Let's consider another example. Maybe you have an issue with envy. When friends describe their new laptops, beach houses, or jobs, you smile politely but can't even hear them because you're consumed with resentment. *I deserve a new job, the latest tech gadget, and a vacation getaway!* At the other end of the envy spectrum, you might tend to belittle yourself and deem yourself unworthy of nice things. Consider this adapted version of Agur's prayer:

Give me neither hateful jealousy nor tiresome self-deprecation,
     but give me self-respect and appreciation for the good
          fortune of others.
Otherwise, I may wall myself off from opportunity
     and say, "How can God possibly use me?"
Or I may turn to spite and bitterness,
     and so dishonor the name of my God.

Can you see how there might also be a sweet spot for how you react to the gifts, talents, and possessions of others? A touch of envy might compel you to venture out of your comfort zone, work a bit harder, and amplify your own gifts. An abundance of envy, however, darkens your heart and inhibits healthy human interaction. To find a good balance, you might consider spending time on a mission field or working with the homeless. The best way to combat envy is to recognize how good you have it.

The overarching point is that your vulnerability—whatever it is—might really be an opportunity, a chance to harness your weakness and make it a strength.

When you identify and zero in on that God-given personality trait, you will start to see the potential for stunning victory. Like so many open doors, you won't race through in an instant. There's a process:

- Step 1: Make sure you don't allow that trait to devolve into a self-destructive extreme of too much or too little.
- Step 2: See that facet of your life as a gift, and assess ways to harness it for good.
- Step 3: Empower friends or family members to nudge you when you drift away from your sweet spot.
- Step 4: Notice others with the same character trait, and come alongside them. You might be the right person to help them avoid the extremes and take full advantage of their power.

Like Agur, if you trust God with your weakness, you just might find a satisfying symmetry for your life.

Whether you're slothful or a workaholic, ask God to help you find that sweet spot balance of work and rest. If you're a control freak, you'll want to find a career path or avocation that requires an impassioned organizer, but ask the Lord to help you consciously let some things slide once in a while. Maybe you have a troubled relationship with food, leaning toward either deprivation or over-indulgence. That's a tough one, but with God's help, you can find a healthy balance.

No one is saying it's always easy to live in contentment with who you are and in every circumstance. From the outside looking in, moderation may even seem boring. But it's not at all. In fact, it's freeing—especially when you invite God to help you find your sweet spot. Expect to find joy in having things just right.

Whichever character trait causes you to transgress, there may be a constant push and pull against extremes. Like Agur, you'll want to identify when and where you are most likely to feel Satan's tug. In some cases, you may want to solicit help from a counselor, accountability partner, pastor, or trusted family member.

When you find your balance, continue to pray for God's protection. Pray that you never forget Satan's seductive power, because he is always just around the corner. But pray also to cast your cares on the Lord. Trust Him for shelter in any emotional storm. Trust Him for your daily bread.

This is God's sweet spot for your life.

The last two chapters of this little book expand on the benefit and bonus of living in that sweet spot. But before that, let's finish our eye-opening exploration of Proverbs 30.

After the Prayer

Do not slander a servant to their master,
　　or they will curse you, and you will pay for it.

There are those who curse their fathers
　　and do not bless their mothers;
those who are pure in their own eyes
　　and yet are not cleansed of their filth;
those whose eyes are ever so haughty,
　　whose glances are so disdainful;
those whose teeth are swords
　　and whose jaws are set with knives
to devour the poor from the earth
　　and the needy from among mankind.

The leech has two daughters.
　　"Give! Give!" they cry.

—PROVERBS 30:10–15

C hapter 30 of Proverbs could end there. As could this book. But Agur chose to continue and so shall we.

When he finishes his thought-provoking prayer, Agur is only one-third of the way through his heavenly writing assignment.

What more is there to say? Well, at this point in biblical history, Agur may very well have read many of the proverbs written by King Solomon. They were organized into chapters and verses centuries later, but you can be sure those nuggets of wisdom were being passed around ancient Jerusalem—mostly by word of mouth. I can imagine Agur studying the words of the wise king and then trying out some of the same literary techniques. That includes metaphors, personification, hyperbole, riddles, euphemisms, parallel constructions, and numerical lists.

Agur does have more to say. And, it turns out, more worth listening to, even three thousand years later. First and foremost, Agur wants to make sure that no serious reader of the Bible glosses over his humble prayer.

Without wasting any time, Agur describes five different choices that can easily sidetrack people from the truth. We slander coworkers. We dishonor parents. We judge others while justifying our own shortcomings. We haughtily look down our noses—even speaking disdainfully—regarding the poor. And all the while, we cry and whine for more . . . and even more.

Can you see how those very human attitudes—vanity, contempt, greed—are the opposite of Agur's prayer? Humility is what allows us to trust God and keeps us on the straight path instead of careening from side to side. When we focus on our own relationship with a trustworthy God, there's no reason to blame, dishonor, castigate, or disparage those around us.

But when we show signs of self-importance and stop trusting God, we allow ourselves to be tempted by lies and distracted by our earthly desires and we start to panic. That's what we get for leaving God's sweet spot.

Here's another way to look at it. If we're busy judging others, we're very likely going to miss our own worthwhile opportunities to do less nasty stuff and more good stuff. Besides, there's only one judge. "God alone, who gave the law, is the Judge. He alone has the power to save or to destroy. So what right do you have to judge your neighbor?" (James 4:12, NLT).

So Agur immediately follows up his prayer with a reminder to spend less time judging others and more time working on our own humility.

After that good word, Agur wraps up his chapter in Proverbs with five short lists. These lists—verses 15–33—read like notes jotted down by a comedian specializing in observational humor.

"Did you ever notice . . ."

"Did you ever wonder about . . ."

"Let me tell you a few things that really bother me . . ."

Again, there are five curious and intriguing lists. Let's take the
next five short chapters to look at them one at a time.

List #1

Things Never Satisfied

There are three things that are never satisfied,
    four that never say, "Enough!":
the grave, the barren womb,
    land, which is never satisfied with water,
    and fire, which never says, "Enough!"

The eye that mocks a father,
    that scorns an aged mother,
will be pecked out by the ravens of the valley,
    will be eaten by the vultures.

—Proverbs 30:15–17

The first list Agur includes in the final half of his chapter serves as a reality check. Agur wants us to know that he is a shrewd observer of the world in which we live, noting that there are truths we cannot escape. He then gives spiritual, emotional, and physical examples. We can't ignore them or fight them. So we might as well prepare for them.

1. **The grave.** Death is inevitable, but our final destination is not. In light of this spiritual truth, we should live with an awareness that we are not home yet. We have only so much time here on earth, and eternity awaits.

2. **A woman who cannot bear children.** If you know a woman or couple aching for a child, you recognize this emotionally charged situation. As we go through life, we are going to meet people who may look as if they have their act together, but they are carrying a heavy burden. The question we need to ask ourselves is, How can we bring comfort and compassion to friends, neighbors, strangers, and family members who are hurting?

3. **The thirsty land.** Back in middle school science class, you learned about the water cycle. Rain, plants, underground water, rivers, oceans, and clouds all play their part in the endless movement of life-giving water. The water cycle is another example of God's organized creation.

4. **Fire.** Just like soil thirsting for water during the growing season, fire also cannot be satisfied. A raging fire will continue to consume any combustible material in its path. It will never stop on its own.

With this list of insatiable elements, Agur confirms that he has a tight grip on the realities of surviving this world. Death is inescapable, family circumstances can be unsettling, and the demands of the land and the volatile nature of fire reveal that the world is not perfect. Agur may even be reflecting on the opening chapters of Genesis. God had created paradise, even saw that it was good, but humankind was not satisfied. Satan's temptation led to the first sin, which ushered in our broken world.

Then, as he does with three of the five lists, Agur adds a follow-up idea. In this case, he uses hyperbole to confirm another truth. Young people need to respect and listen to their mom and dad. A child best learns truth through the eyes of caring parents. The pecking ravens are most likely a metaphor suggesting that if you mock or disrespect your parents, your worldview turns dark.

Agur gets it. He understands the ways of the spiritual world, the physical world, and human relations. His insight can be trusted.

Three—No, Four?

Of Agur's five lists, four of them begin with a kind of joking aside as if he's playing a game with words and numbers. He composes these curious lists to make a point about God's creation, including geology, zoology, physics, and human nature.

Each list has only four items. But he wants the reader to know that each list could conceivably go on for several pages. He says, "There are three things, no, actually four . . ." That wordplay invites readers to use their own imaginations to envision other examples of mysteries, mistakes, and marvels.

In other words, the Bible isn't something you just read. It's meant to be experienced, pondered, and applied to everyday life.

List #2

Amazing Enigmas

There are three things that are too amazing for me,
>   four that I do not understand:
the way of an eagle in the sky,
>   the way of a snake on a rock,
the way of a ship on the high seas,
>   and the way of a man with a young woman.

This is the way of an adulterous woman:
>   She eats and wipes her mouth
>   and says, "I've done nothing wrong."

—PROVERBS 30:18–20

Agur's second list confirms that God's ways are beyond human imagination. And that's the way it should be. I don't know about you, but I prefer a God who has a better handle than me on how things work.

When we stop and think about God's design for the natural world, it should blow our minds. Isaiah 55:8–9 explains that we can seek to know God, but we can never truly understand who He is and how He carries out His plan:

"My thoughts are not your thoughts,
    neither are your ways my ways,"
        declares the LORD.
"As the heavens are higher than the earth,
    so are my ways higher than your ways,
    and my thoughts than your thoughts."

Agur gives us four examples of how the Creator of the universe works in ways we may never understand.

1. How an eagle flies
2. How a snake moves
3. How boats stay afloat
4. How God designed attraction, love, romance, sex, and procreation

With this list, Agur reveals his appreciation for God's design when it comes to biology, physics, and human nature. Most of us have been transfixed by the sweeping arc of an eagle in flight. Snakes have been creepily crawling on their bellies since Eden. Boat builders in ancient Israel knew how to build a seaworthy boat, but they probably weren't calculating buoyancy forces and the physical properties of water displacement. Once again, Agur reveals his sense of humor and speaks to every future generation when he confesses that men really don't know what women want.

After listing those four amazing enigmas, Agur tackles an issue that might not be so mysterious. As can be found in many chapters in Proverbs, he offers a verse with a condemning tone that seems to come out of nowhere, perhaps to address an issue that he has seen tearing apart families and communities.

Agur reports that a prostitute can commit an adulterous act and completely deny that she has sinned. That tendency to deny culpability when we have done something wrong is woven into our humanity. Cain denied his role in the first murder and was banished from paradise. In Titus 1:16, we read about people who "claim to know God, but by their actions they deny him. They are detestable, disobedient and unfit for doing anything good." Even Peter denied Christ, but his immediate contrition and repentance rescued him from God's wrath and secured his place as a leader in the early church.

By highlighting these enigmas, Agur confirms that God has an all-encompassing, well-ordered design for our world that the human mind cannot grasp. We should not expect to understand God, and we can trust that His plan for our lives is far better than we could imagine ourselves.

List #3

Human Mistakes

Under three things the earth trembles,
under four it cannot bear up:
a servant who becomes king
a godless fool who gets plenty to eat
a contemptible woman who gets married,
and a servant who displaces her mistress.

—PROVERBS 30:21–23

While Agur focuses mostly on science for the first two lists, he turns to significant blunders of human nature for list number three.

So often we turn our backs on God, believing we have a better plan. As a result, the earth trembles. Agur may not be talking about literal earthquakes here, but he is saying God's steadfast plan provides balance or equilibrium. It makes sense. First Corinthians 14:33 confirms, "God is not the author of confusion but of peace" (NKJV).

1. **Experience matters.** When an untrained servant is put in charge, chaos follows. Certainly, an ambitious young man or woman can study, work, and advance through the ranks in a company or kingdom. But that arduous process takes time, allowing for the establishment of expectations and a foundation of competence and maturity. Skipping from the role of servant directly to the role of king would be a lose-lose for all involved.

2. **Gluttony kills.** When people get everything they want without working, they have no motivation, no

responsibilities, and no reliance on God. Consider the dismal fate of most lottery winners. Unearned wealth is a burden few can handle. Similarly, if your parents leave you a fortune, be warned. Don't spend your days lounging around the pool or your nights throwing wild parties. Consider the lesson of the prodigal son (see Luke 15:11–32).

3. **Love wins.** A marriage without love is destined to fail. Of course, every marriage will go through seasons of highs and lows. And love can be difficult to define. But consider this warning *before* the engagement: Don't marry for spite, lust, or greed. Don't marry out of convenience, practicality, or to escape your parents. Marry because you can't imagine living without that person.

4. **Adultery destroys.** Honoring and protecting marriage are also the focus of the fourth item on this list. In Agur's day—and even today—wedding vows might be forgotten when temptation looms near. Consider this a warning to all married men and women to be especially careful of giving undue attention (e.g., flirting) to coworkers and others in your sphere of influence.

Agur is not covering new ground here. The undeniable benefits of following God's guidance are sprinkled throughout Proverbs and all of Scripture. There are clear moral values to uphold as well as evidence for absolute right and wrong. Nevertheless, don't panic when you or a loved one strays from the path of righteousness. Human mistakes may cause the earth to tremble but not to crumble. God will always make room for a repentant sinner.

Agur is simply reminding us there is a better plan. And we can know it. If your choices align with God's perfect plan when it comes to climbing social ranks, earning your daily bread, marrying for love, and keeping the marriage bed pure, well done. Thinking back to the overarching lesson of Agur's prayer, your ongoing assignment is to consider your own areas of weakness, find your sweet spot, and build your foundation on solid biblical footing.

List #4

Small Wonders

Four things on earth are small,
>   yet they are extremely wise:
Ants are creatures of little strength,
>   yet they store up their food in the summer;
hyraxes are creatures of little power,
>   yet they make their home in the crags;
locusts have no king,
>   yet they advance together in ranks;
a lizard can be caught with the hand,
>   yet it is found in kings' palaces.

—PROVERBS 30:24–28

Ants, hyraxes, locusts, and lizards are the stars of Agur's next list. What can we possibly learn from these small creatures? How about this? These brilliantly designed critters all take full advantage of the limited gifts granted them by the Creator.

1. **Ants wisely store food in bulk for the winter.**

   According to an article by Ohio State researchers in the *Journal of Biomechanics,*[9] ants can lift up to five thousand times their body weight before their necks rupture and their heads pop off.[10] Agur didn't have an electron microscope or micro-CT scanner to calculate that number, but he was inspired by God to recognize that the ants' diminutive size doesn't define their potency. Ants effectively use the abilities they have to prepare for the needs of tomorrow.

2. **The clever hyrax takes refuge in hillside crags.**

   Hyraxes, huh? The hyrax is the cutest little creature you've ever not seen. Go ahead, search online, find a photo or two, and prepare to smile. The Old Testament

gives them several shout-outs. Leviticus and Deuteronomy note that the cud-chewing hyrax is unclean,[11]
while David mentions that the crags provide refuge
for them.[12] Also called coneys, rock badgers, and
shephanim, these cute little guys spend most of their
time sunbathing on narrow cliffs but quickly scamper
into mountain crevices when danger appears. For you
and me, the reminder is obvious. We also have a rock
in which to hide. Second Samuel 22:2 says it well: "The
LORD is my rock, my fortress and my deliverer." Even
as we bask in His provision, let's not wander too far
from His protection.

3. **Locusts have no leaders, yet they spread terror and
destruction quite effectively.** The lesson of the locust
might be to acknowledge the power of many individuals
working together. Conversely, Agur might be warning
us that unguided mob action leads to rampant carnage.
Or maybe he's giving Bible readers a reminder of the
plagues of Egypt or a foreshadowing of the nasty locusts
(or evil spirits) described in Revelation who will be sent
to devour all those without the seal of God.[13] As a
prophet, Agur might have had the ability to see that
far into the future.

4. **Lizards sneak into castles.** Agur paints a humorous
picture here. Imagine hulking palace guards bumping
into one another as they try to catch a scampering

lizard. I think Agur might be telling us not to take ourselves too seriously and not to panic when minor details don't go our way. After all, even powerful kings cannot stop lizards from scampering around their homes. Or maybe Agur is reinforcing the main lesson of this list: don't take small things for granted.

List #5

The Downfall of Kings

There are three things that are stately in their stride,
    four that move with stately bearing:
a lion, mighty among beasts,
    who retreats before nothing;
a strutting rooster, a he-goat,
    and a king secure against revolt.

If you play the fool and exalt yourself,
    or if you plan evil,
    clap your hand over your mouth!
For as churning cream produces butter,
    and as twisting the nose produces blood,
    so stirring up anger produces strife.

—Proverbs 30:29–33

gur's final list presents four images of those who seemingly stand tall, all of whom might be on the verge of a fall. Questions come to mind. As kings of their individual domains, what are their responsibilities? Who made them kings? And do earthly kingdoms last forever?

1. The lion, roaring king of beasts
2. The rooster, crowing king of the barnyard
3. The male goat, braying king of the mountain
4. A king with so many armies and weapons that he believes he is invincible

That short list of boastful kings is followed by wise words for all those who foolishly exalt themselves. Even if lions, roosters, goats, and arrogant kings miss the lesson, it's still valuable to us. No matter how powerful you are, when you act rudely, stir up anger, or actively plan evil, then you should know what's coming. It won't be pleasant, and you probably deserve it.

In the final two verses, Agur clearly describes a frequent source of human strife and turmoil. Whether it's cataclysmic or quietly unsettling, much of our conflict is the result of that classic human stumbling block: pride. Or, more accurately, destructive pride.

The way to counteract destructive pride is to practice submissive humility. Admitting our reliance on God is a recurring theme of Agur's chapter and a character trait valued throughout Scripture.

"Let the one who boasts boast in the Lord." For it is not the one who commends himself who is approved, but the one whom the Lord commends. (2 Corinthians 10:17–18)

ABOUT THE WORD PRIDE

Unfortunately, the English language uses the same word for haughty arrogance as it does for the feeling of accomplishment that comes from working hard and achieving a goal. It's really okay to feel proud after you finish rebricking your patio, have a poem published, or win the Nobel Peace Prize. If you're a parent, I hope you do feel parental pride when your kid wins a spelling bee, graduates from a trade school, or swishes a three-pointer at the buzzer to clinch a playoff berth.

Let's all agree not to discourage feelings of uplifting pride just because the other kind of pride can be so destructive.

Pride goes before destruction, a haughty spirit before a fall. (Proverbs 16:18)

Do nothing out of selfish ambition or vain conceit. Rather, in humility value others above yourselves. (Philippians 2:3)

Humble yourselves before the Lord, and he will lift you up. (James 4:10)

This should leave us with a significant realization. Like the lion, rooster, goat, and arrogant king, we have each been given our own kingdom to watch over and maintain. But unlike those earthly kings, you are smart enough to realize you are dependent on God.

The Creator provided the territory over which you reign, and He has established a purpose and plans unique to you. In order for those plans to come to fruition, God Himself has showered you with gifts, resources, and wisdom (some still waiting to be discovered). Every one of us is different. None of us is more important than anyone else. But make no mistake: your personal kingdom requires you to be your best self. God is calling you because there is work to do.

Don't panic over that responsibility. Rejoice and accept the challenge. Self-proclaimed kings are destined to fall. But you were given authority by the King of kings, which means you are destined for greatness.

Consider again the lessons of Agur's five lists: the physical world has limits, there are mysteries we cannot understand, humans err, details matter, and even earthly kings need to remember that this world is not our home.

We'll take two more chapters to wrap up this little book, looking one more time at the Prayer of Agur. Then it's time for each of us to triumphantly reign over our personal kingdom in light of eternity.

14

Life in the Sweet Spot

Two things I ask of you, Lord;
    do not refuse me before I die:
Keep falsehood and lies far from me;
    give me neither poverty nor riches,
    but give me only my daily bread.
Otherwise, I may have too much and disown you
    and say, "Who is the Lord?"
Or I may become poor and steal,
    and so dishonor the name of my God.

—Proverbs 30:7–9

As you can see, there's more to Proverbs 30 than most people realize: Prophecy we can trust. Opportunities to deepen our faith. Quirky insights from a creative list maker. You also may have discovered a personal assignment or two.

But the heart of Agur's singular chapter can be found in his prayer: to evade the lies and temptations of this world and trust God to provide our daily needs. God's answers to those two requests should keep us running on a straight track down the middle of the road, not banging off the guardrails.

So, are you living in God's sweet spot? Or are you forever destined to live on the fringe? Do you really want to continue suffering through money woes, anger issues, a self-esteem drought, raging jealousy, aimless purpose, or other extremes that sabotage your best life?

Hmmm.

Why was it that you picked up this book and read all the way to the end?

You were hoping to find your own sweet spot, right? Admittedly, the last several pages referencing snakes, lizards, eagles, and lions may have seemed like a distraction. But we covered some important ground. Agur delivered wise and worthy counsel on esteeming God's design, maintaining a healthy marriage, respecting your parents, and keeping your pride in check. Digging into Scripture is always beneficial. But let's get back to the idea of living in that sweet spot God has specifically for you.

It's quite possible that you still may not recognize the full advantage of living in God's sweet spot. For one thing, you may assume that aiming for a life of contentment is a compromise or an excuse not to work toward your full potential. In fact, the opposite is true! Living in the sweet spot with God is empowering. For example, a healthy life equilibrium is the perfect place from which to launch a business, finish your education, or fall in love.

How's that? Any new business you start will require a harmonious balance of creative ambition and realistic expectations. To go back to school, you need self-determination and an ambitious timeline but also a good grasp on reality that leaves room for life's inevitable interruptions. To find your soul mate, you're going to have to courageously put your best self out there while making yourself vulnerable to possibly having your heart broken.

Praying the prayer of Agur leads to patience when things aren't moving fast enough and composure when things get a little out of control. Never forget, the goal is to find that balance between too much and too little.

In God's sweet spot, the pressure is off. Really. You can be sure it's all going to work out. You are not required to start a business this year, enroll for school next semester, look for love, or tackle any other ambitious endeavor. But why not go for it? Otherwise, you're just sitting on the sidelines, and that's not sweet at all.

Perhaps the best thing about living in God's sweet spot is that you can move forward to explore life, secure in your relationship with the Creator of the universe. When you find yourself panicking over worldly successes or failures, it's reassuring to know God loves you no matter what. This is true when you're on a winning streak or when you're hurting. When you're seeking His face or turning away. Whether your cup is empty or overflowing. The fact that God loves you *just as you are* is the truest thing about you.

God isn't impressed with your Rolex watch, washboard abs, trophy spouse, or even your million-dollar gift to charity.

In much the same way, from God's perspective it's okay if your lawn has a few dandelions, your car has some rust spots, or you don't get into Harvard. He wants you to be okay with it too.

In that sweet spot—when you choose to depend on God's guidance and provision—your most important activity is to lean into God. Keep listening. Expect clear instruction. We're promised in James 4:8, "Draw near to God and He will draw near to you" (NKJV).

As you increasingly choose to depend on God alone for your daily needs, you become more like Him. Your ability to know right from wrong sharpens. The extremes become less attractive. As you walk that straight path, you cherish today and anticipate tomorrow. The right doors open, and aggravating obstacles vanish.

The true benefits of Agur's prayer will then become clear. Your boring, narrow, straight-down-the-middle path *leads you to your purpose:* doing great things and finding joy-filled satisfaction.

Suddenly, you'll find yourself experiencing the Sweet Spot Bonus.

15

The Sweet Spot Bonus

I know that there is nothing better for people than
to be happy and to do good while they live. That each
of them may eat and drink, and find satisfaction in all
their toil—this is the gift of God.

—ECCLESIASTES 3:12–13

This little book has one more twist. It's a universal—and quite wonderful—secret for all those who follow God, yet most people miss it.

To reveal that secret, we're going to leave Agur's prayer and flip ahead from the last pages of Proverbs to the opening pages of the very next book in the Bible, Ecclesiastes.

You'll immediately recognize this passage. It's Solomon's own version of "How to Live in God's Sweet Spot." Ecclesiastes 3 reminds us that no matter what you are going through, the exact opposite is just around the corner. For example, right now you may find yourself crying, speaking up, or holding tight to something precious. But before long you can expect to be laughing, staying silent, or letting go of a long-held treasure.

There is a time for everything,
    and a season for every activity under the heavens:

    a time to be born and a time to die,
    a time to plant and a time to uproot,

a time to kill and a time to heal,

a time to tear down and a time to build,

a time to weep and a time to laugh,

a time to mourn and a time to dance,

a time to scatter stones and a time to gather them,

a time to embrace and a time to refrain from embracing,

a time to search and a time to give up,

a time to keep and a time to throw away,

a time to tear and a time to mend,

a time to be silent and a time to speak,

a time to love and a time to hate,

a time for war and a time for peace. (Ecclesiastes 3:1–8)

This well-loved portion of Scripture—like the Prayer of Agur—asks you to trust God. Nothing surprises Him. Every season is part of His plan. He has work for you to do, but you can be sure He is going to work all things out for good.

Right after this passage, Solomon follows up his list of seasons with three wonderfully relevant observations inspired by God. Look again at the two Scripture verses that begin this chapter. You'll find three action items: Be happy. Do good. Find satisfaction.

Be. Do. Find.

Those activities are not burdens; they're gifts! You receive them when you finally anchor yourself in God's sweet spot. At that critical moment, God will reveal your assignment. You will discover the life-changing projects only you can do.

Does that scare you? It should not. Because God equips those He calls. As a matter of fact, He already has been preparing you to meet the challenge. Ephesians 2:10 expresses it well: "We are his workmanship, created in Christ Jesus for good works, which God prepared beforehand, that we should walk in them" (ESV).

With that in mind, here's the bonus available to anyone seeking God's face. It's the answer to the proverbial question, "What should I do?"

You will not be surprised to hear it's about balance. God is not asking you to career back and forth down a dark, unfamiliar highway without GPS, headlights, or brakes.

Listen now. *God wants you to do stuff that comes easily.* If you can dance, dance. If you can write, write. If you can build, build. If you can plant, plant. If you can hug, hug.

Does that sound obvious? Too many people miss this point. They find listening to God and following His plan bewildering, as if God would want us to be confused. They think working for God is tedious, unfulfilling, and backbreaking, as if God would want us to be miserable.

Why is that? Maybe every interaction they've had with God or church has been boring or painful. Maybe they were taught to live in fear of a God who delivers only judgment and wrath. Maybe they think that if something is easy or personally gratifying, it's not worth doing. Maybe no one ever challenged them to chase their dreams. Worse, maybe their dreams were mocked or written off as impractical.

It's true that God will often ask you to step out of your comfort zone. He wants you to stretch yourself, to dig deep and do great things. On your life journey, there may even be some dark tunnels, brambles, and detours along the way. But you can trust He has specifically equipped you to overcome every obstacle. When you look back at just about any difficult season of life, you'll realize that meeting and overcoming those trials actually left you stronger, wiser, and filled with a sense of achievement and new confidence. Never were you outside His sovereignty and loving care.

So here is your challenge: Do not be someone who perpetually sets aside activities you enjoy because you think you're not worthy or you need to earn the right to be happy. Do not wait any longer for the stars to align before you follow your sweetest dreams. Consider the possibility that you can live in God's sweet spot this very day.

Remember, you are God's workmanship. He has been preparing you for specific good works since before you were born. Recognize and believe that what you enjoy—your natural giftedness—is a gift you can give back to God.

In other words, don't exhaust yourself with sweat and study trying to be good at something you don't care about. Instead, put your best efforts into something you're already good at, and then commit your heart, mind, and soul to take it to the next level.

Consider for a moment people you know—friends or heroes—who excel at what they do. From the outside looking in, it seems as if everything they do is effortless. How do they do that? Well, maybe it's because they have devoted their lives to activities that come easily to them. They're simply embracing their gifts.

Whether they know it or not, most successful people have discovered the Sweet Spot Bonus. Now it's your turn.

Open your eyes, heart, mind, and soul to what you already know. Be who you are. Claim your title as the one person in the world uniquely designed to be you.

Do what you do best. Do it with excellence. And get ready to give God the glory.

Heavenly Father, help me see with clarity and walk in the light of Your truth. Keep me from extremes where I am no longer seeking Your face. Give me only my daily bread that I might depend only on You, experiencing contentment, composure, and appreciation. Establish in me harmony, balance, and trust that I might serve You with a joy-filled confidence, shining the light of Your love and truth into dark corners of this world. Help me love You, myself, and others well. As I trust You, reveal opportunities for me to use those gifts You have so generously given me—guiding me to the right places, projects, and people. I give You all the glory as I seek to live in that sweet spot found in the center of Your will here and for eternity. In Your worthy name, I pray. Amen.

Proverbs 30

The sayings of Agur son of Jakeh—an inspired utterance.

This man's utterance to Ithiel:

"I am weary, God,
   but I can prevail.
Surely I am only a brute, not a man;
   I do not have human understanding.
I have not learned wisdom,
   nor have I attained to the knowledge of the Holy One.
Who has gone up to heaven and come down?
   Whose hands have gathered up the wind?
Who has wrapped up the waters in a cloak?
   Who has established all the ends of the earth?
What is his name, and what is the name of his son?
   Surely you know!

"Every word of God is flawless;
   he is a shield to those who take refuge in him.
Do not add to his words,
   or he will rebuke you and prove you a liar.

"Two things I ask of you, LORD;
   do not refuse me before I die:

Keep falsehood and lies far from me;
    give me neither poverty nor riches,
    but give me only my daily bread.
Otherwise, I may have too much and disown you
    and say, 'Who is the Lord?'
Or I may become poor and steal,
    and so dishonor the name of my God.

"Do not slander a servant to their master,
    or they will curse you, and you will pay for it.

"There are those who curse their fathers
    and do not bless their mothers;
those who are pure in their own eyes
    and yet are not cleansed of their filth;
those whose eyes are ever so haughty,
    whose glances are so disdainful;
those whose teeth are swords
    and whose jaws are set with knives
to devour the poor from the earth
    and the needy from among mankind.

"The leech has two daughters.
    'Give! Give!' they cry.

"There are three things that are never satisfied,
    four that never say, 'Enough!':
the grave, the barren womb,

land, which is never satisfied with water,
    and fire, which never says, 'Enough!'

"The eye that mocks a father,
    that scorns an aged mother,
will be pecked out by the ravens of the valley,
    will be eaten by the vultures.

"There are three things that are too amazing for me,
    four that I do not understand:
the way of an eagle in the sky,
    the way of a snake on a rock,
the way of a ship on the high seas,
    and the way of a man with a young woman.

"This is the way of an adulterous woman:
    She eats and wipes her mouth
    and says, 'I've done nothing wrong.'

"Under three things the earth trembles,
    under four it cannot bear up:
a servant who becomes king,
    a godless fool who gets plenty to eat,
a contemptible woman who gets married,
    and a servant who displaces her mistress.

"Four things on earth are small,
    yet they are extremely wise:

Ants are creatures of little strength,
    yet they store up their food in the summer;
hyraxes are creatures of little power,
    yet they make their home in the crags;
locusts have no king,
    yet they advance together in ranks;
a lizard can be caught with the hand,
    yet it is found in kings' palaces.

"There are three things that are stately in their stride,
    four that move with stately bearing:
a lion, mighty among beasts,
    who retreats before nothing;
a strutting rooster, a he-goat,
    and a king secure against revolt.

"If you play the fool and exalt yourself,
    or if you plan evil,
    clap your hand over your mouth!
For as churning cream produces butter,
    and as twisting the nose produces blood,
    so stirring up anger produces strife."

Questions for Personal Reflection or Small Group Discussion

Introduction

1. How did you discover this book?
2. Have you previously given any thought to Agur or his prayer in Proverbs 30:7–9?
3. Describe a season of life in which you felt as though you were in balance—in a sweet spot. Or a time when you unexpectedly lost your balance.

Chapter 1: Major Impact from a Minor Character

1. What life lesson have you learned from a biblical character?
2. What life lesson have you learned from someone just passing through your life?
3. When was the last time you saw yourself as a skeptic, cynic, or seeker?

Chapter 2: Utterance from a Collector

1. In this world, which is a more valuable attribute: humility or overconfidence? Which is more dangerous?
2. Why should we listen to someone who confesses he does not have "human understanding" and has "not learned wisdom"?

3. It might be mere speculation, but how do you think a guy like Agur earned a spot in the Bible?

Chapter 3: Agur Asks Questions Worth Asking

1. Name a question to which you could answer "Surely I know!"
2. Currently, what is your source of confidence?
3. How do you think Agur's contemporaries reacted when he implied that God has a Son?

Chapter 4: Agur Takes a Moment to Endorse Scripture

1. Why do you think the author of a single chapter in the Bible would include a personal endorsement of the Bible?
2. Are doubts evil?
3. How do you personally know the Bible is true?

Chapter 5: Agur's Prayer, Part I: Regarding Lies Coming and Going

1. Describe your prayer life. How might lengthy prayers trip you up?
2. What's more dangerous: hearing lies or telling lies?
3. How would you answer the question "What is truth?"

Chapter 6: Agur's Prayer, Part II: Not Too Much, Not Too Little

1. What's a bigger challenge: having too much or having too little?

2. Compare the idea of a "sweet spot" to "daily bread." How are they similar or different?

3. Which way is our society headed today: toward minimalism or overconsumption?

Chapter 7: Agur's Prayer, Part III: Possible Repercussions of Living in the Extremes

1. Do you have an emotional attachment to money?

2. Several Scripture verses in this chapter affirm Agur's prayer. Which will you remember?

3. Is it reasonable to take Agur's prayer for a financial sweet spot and apply it to other temptations and vulnerabilities?

Chapter 8: After the Prayer

1. Agur lists a few not-so-nice habits. Can you relate to any of them?

2. Are you quick to judge others? What might be another option?

3. Has Agur earned your trust? Or do you see him as he described himself—as a brute of a man who has not learned wisdom?

Chapter 9: List #1: Things Never Satisfied

1. Are you ready for the inevitable grave?

2. When was the last time you set aside your own agenda to help a hurting family member or friend?

3. How are you honoring your mother and father?

Chapter 10: List #2: Amazing Enigmas

1. Do you take God's design for this world for granted?
2. Have you taken the necessary steps to protect your heart and mind from adultery?
3. When is the last time you covered up a mistake or misdeed with the words "I've done nothing wrong"?

Chapter 11: List #3: Human Mistakes

1. Why would the earth tremble because of mere human mistakes?
2. Can you restate the lessons on leadership, moderation, and marriage?
3. What should your response be to biblical instruction?

Chapter 12: List #4: Small Wonders

1. Can you relate best to the lesson of the ants, hyraxes, locusts, or lizards?
2. What small thing in your life—whether frustration or opportunity—might be worthy of your full attention?
3. What gift, experience, or talent from your past that seemed trivial at the time might be worth reassessing?

Chapter 13: List #5: The Downfall of Kings

1. Do you have a kingdom?
2. What's the opposite of destructive pride?

3. Which of Agur's five lists left you with the most compelling personal insight?

Chapter 14: Life in the Sweet Spot

1. Do you see God's sweet spot as a compromise or a firm foundation for launching your next season of life?
2. What's the next big thing in your life, and what are the extremes you need to avoid?
3. What is the truest thing about you?

Chapter 15: The Sweet Spot Bonus

1. Before picking up this book, many readers were unfamiliar with Proverbs 30 but quite familiar with Ecclesiastes 3. Can you relate?
2. The mandate of the Sweet Spot Bonus is to be happy, do good, and find satisfaction. Which of those three directives do you find most difficult?
3. Name three activities that come easily to you, bring joy, and might be the key to finding your sweet spot.
4. When you find yourself in the center of God's will and checking off achievements that matter, to whom will you give the glory?

Notes

1. Rev. J. W. Nutt, "Proverbs 30," in *Ellicott's Commentary for English Readers,* ed. Charles John Ellicott, 1905, https://biblehub.com/commentaries/ellicott/proverbs /30.htm.

2. M. G. Easton, *Illustrated Bible Dictionary,* 3rd ed. (Nashville: Thomas Nelson, 1897), s.v. "Agur," www.biblestudy tools.com/dictionaries/eastons-bible-dictionary/agur.html.

3. James Orr, ed., *International Standard Bible Encyclopedia* (1915), s.v. "Jakeh," www.biblestudytools.com/dictionary /jakeh.

4. Scholarly sources consulted include James Strong, *New Strong's Exhaustive Concordance* (Nashville: Thomas Nelson, 2003); and Matthew Poole, *A Commentary on the Holy Bible* (London, ON: Macdonald, 1985).

5. See Isaiah 9:6–7; Daniel 3:25; Hosea 11:1; Micah 5:1–3.

6. Adam Simnowitz, "Son of God in the Old Testament," Biblical Missiology, February 11, 2013, http://biblical missiology.org/2013/02/11/son-of-god-in-the-old-testament.

7. Rev. R. Payne Smith, "Genesis 21," in *Ellicott's Commentary for English Readers,* ed. Charles John Ellicott, 1905, bible hub.com/commentaries/ellicott/genesis/21.htm.

8. Popularized by Pope Gregory the Great in the sixth century, the seven deadly sins were taught to all laypeople throughout the Middle Ages. For more information on their origins and history, visit www.deadlysins.com/history.

9. Vienny Nguyen, Blaine Lilly, and Carlos Castro, "The Exoskeletal Structure and Tensile Loading Behavior of an Ant Neck Joint," *Journal of Biomechanics* 47, no. 2 (January 22, 2014): 497–504, www.sciencedirect.com/science/article/pii/S0021929013005459.

10. "Ants Can Lift Up to 5,000 Times Their Own Body Weight," Entomology Today, February 11, 2014, https://entomologytoday.org/2014/02/11/ants-can-lift-up-to-5000-times-their-own-body-weight-new-study-suggests.

11. See Leviticus 11:5; Deuteronomy 14:7.

12. See Psalm 104:18.

13. To read the story of Moses, Aaron, and the plagues in Egypt, see Exodus 7:1–12:42. For the mention of locusts in John's vision, see Revelation 9:3–7.

About the Author

Jay Payleitner spent a decade in major-market advertising on Chicago's Michigan Avenue. Following God's clear call, Jay served two decades as a freelance radio producer working with Josh McDowell, Chuck Colson, TobyMac, Bible League International, National Center for Fathering, and others. He's a national speaker on marriage, parenting, and getting life right. Most notably, Jay has written more than twenty-five books, including *52 Things Kids Need from a Dad, What If God Wrote Your Bucket List?* and *The Jesus Dare.* His books have been translated into nine languages and have sold more than a half-million copies. He has been a guest multiple times on *The Harvest Show,* Moody Radio, and *Focus on the Family.* Jay and his high school sweetheart, Rita, live in St. Charles, Illinois, where they raised five awesome kids, loved on ten foster babies, and are cherishing grandparenthood. Track him down at jaypayleitner.com.